THIS TREMOR LOVE IS

THIS TREMOR LOVE IS

Daphne Marlatt

Talonbooks

Talonbooks
P.O. Box 2076, Vancouver, British Columbia, Canada V6B 3S3
www.talonbooks.com

Typeset in Adobe Garamond and printed and bound in Canada.

Second Printing: 2008

The publisher gratefully acknowledges the financial support of the Canada Council for the Arts; the Government of Canada through the Book Publishing Industry Development Program; and the Province of British Columbia through the British Columbia Arts Council for our publishing activities.

National Library of Canada Cataloguing in Publication Data

Marlatt, Daphne, 1942-
  This tremor love is

  Poems.
  ISBN 0-88922-450-1

  I. Title.
  PS8576.A74T54 2001   C811'.54   C2001-910189-9
  PR9199.3.M36T54 2001

  ISBN-13: 978-0-88922-450-6

ACKNOWLEDGEMENTS

The author wishes to thank The British Columbia Arts Council and The Canada Council for financial assistance during the writing of this book.

Heartfelt thanks to Bridget MacKenzie, Roy Kiyooka, and Betsy Warland for inspiration and companionship, as well as to the many writers, named and unnamed in these pages, whose work has formed a stimulating matrix for this collection. In particular, deep gratitude to Zasep Tulku Rinpoche for profound teachings beyond the limits of this writing.

Special thanks to Karl Siegler for thoughtful editing and to Talonbooks for actively supporting poetry for so many years.

Thanks also to Christine Hobbs at the National Library and Ralph Stanton at Simon Fraser University's Special Collections for their help in researching sources.

Some of these poems, some in earlier versions (and occasionally under different titles), have appeared in: *The Capilano Review, Grain, West Coast Line, Poetrywales, Writing Right* (ed. Doug Barbour & Marni Stanley, Longspoon Press, 1982) & *Kitchen Talk* (ed. Edna Alford & Claire Harris, Red Deer College Press, 1992). The first three poems were published by Mona Fertig & Peter Haase as a work of book art, *Winter/Rice/Tea Strain*, ((m)Other Tongue Press, 2000). An earlier version of *here & there* first saw light as an Island Writing Series chapbook (1981). "life expectancy" originally appeared, again in earlier version, as a 1980 broadside from Peter and Meredith Quartermain's Slug Press. Earlier versions of "space activities" (originally titled "At Birch Bay"), "where we live" (originally "New Moon") and "listen" appeared in *Net Work: Selected Writing* (ed. Fred Wah, Talonbooks, 1980). "the tri-cornered heart" and "seeing it go up in smoke," as well as "booking passage" were first collected in *Salvage* (Red Deer College Press, 1991).

CONTENTS

A LOST BOOK

(poems 1974-1999)

for Roy

winter/ rice/ tea strain

ocha words

— well into winter,   we stir up out of what,   what dreams,   what
cause of communion,   names,   odd stirrings-up of the past as
honey pours,   *your dream was*   this & this reading, this poem
pouring this cup of tea   proposes (your favourite word)

days stream down any one of the window panes i press my nose against/
you — start & drop the book, your books, all over the floor   *so much
depends*   begin again, pressing these days into pages as if, paged
we could pull out any one to savour — this one so young, these

nouns i want to call out to you   winter/ rice/ tea strain, unlikely
sweet tongue, a green hope i bury my face into, steam's slip, & you
overheard, breathing yourself into sound

touch

the music rice makes, rice on the tongue in our tea, tea & trout, while outside
rain's quintet batters our ears   hardly the bitterest month, sweet steep, sweet
infusion of green   tipping our lips at the smallest ordinary then   crescendo light
through dark your eye
                              stares i stare, in step, the skin of your foot so smooth it
startles, quick

        trout where the darkness lies

                                              unformed its leap mere shine
ichthyic, from the base of the spinal column's chorded ascent (rippling
through the lines of what was planned, unplanned, undone — nothing
to catch our lines haphazard lie

                        gen mai cha grain
                        between the teeth, still i see

you eye luminant, luminous wonder my eye wanders, amazed & touching
touched with *astony*, love, the thunder of it inflorescent you said   a downpour
trout weave through as you described yourself so slow to leap

                                          out in what is

clearly the wonder of budding, leaves, scales of the old
miraculous, adart in the air as a friend would say *among*

bachi

sea bush, "small tree"   fruit-bearing, salt-sprung   fights your big wood
making a world — *poiein* — to its own description these drenched leaves
straining toward the light, spume, drift of repeated observation drawn
to shore

     you offer tea, wipe the wood of the table clearing sea wrack, surface
grit   we sip to a murmuring of visions, yours, mine, inter-inflected

                                     yet to break
our description of the world & thence to see   *the dreamer & the dreamed*   who's
dreaming who? you asked

wind buffets the windowpane   words incessant as rain fall   hear what slips
between   this tea we bring to our different lips, this space where nouns unfold

leaf
    by leaf

       bits on the floor of the pot we disappear

hands on the table

for Edrys (1918-75)

i

hands,   in dream   there are hands,   small   of a child who goes off
into the abyss alone   (hear someone cry?   & stare up into that space
he sleeps at the top of   as if it were visible, this sound — a false
signal, a turning away   he doesn't cry, my five-year old, he sleeps

who cried then?   cried out in sleep, turning   on the other side of
dream   awake, slides easily out & howls in pain of being   here
which is not here, not yet   as there

                                              was a place
where two could jump off the known still holding hands & then?
one was alone?   awake?

you wipe the table bare   there are prints on it   hands that
come up in dream   but not our own

                                    why this? why should i dream of
hands that stay   when you constantly wipe our table clean with care
'thorough' you say, to sit, 'sit at'   you who sit easily separating the
cigarettes, the cup, & thus acknowledging all your habits 'that do not
weigh so much' to make a place we sit down to, bare the table & place
what belongs, so spare, & then make visible, perhaps, that which comes up
out of nothing & lifts us, like a wind, into recognition

14

it was bare, swept clean by fire, & black   a gutted church (the church
she was wedded in, my mother   before the bomb, before the beggars
light falls sideways through what's left of the wall   only a few charred
timbers, only the memory of light, of many hands held up to receive in
supplication, out of need, asking for food, for anything

                                      before
a communion table, there *was* a rail these supplicants knelt at
in engagement, in a vow   ('engagement' had nothing to do with
this interpenetration of light & dark

                        bombed by the time i saw it, & his face
so dark & he so curled apart, like some child, a hand thrust between his
knees in the comfort of sex to ease what must have been always present,
given his bony calves, like sticks, this beggar curled   a child or like a child
where the light falls all around a bombed-out church Sir Francis Light still
stands erect outside of   like some dream in the back of a head, a flicker of
frames casting their imagery of light on the dark remains   who stays or what
inhabits the broken belly of this church   stays on in pain in the dark his hands
press past, eating away at the continuity that says

always there is someone who stays, who keeps faith

always they said, when the image arose, this is the church we were married in, this
is the church of ruin, my image now   she was all in white when they knelt & later
stood on the lawn where the cannon stood & the cannas flared she knelt in the
law & champagne poured though she knew nothing of bed & he wore a white
carnation under his jaw

                        always there is this other who sleeps in the
bombed-out building of my mind   as the wine & wedding were for them
mother & father who stood where they were to become in turn separate
images of the law   as the dream grows always there was this other, a child

a beggar curled in the bombed-out building of their vows   they held hands
& the child in the dark of the dream grew   the more they held, they held
on

iii

it was a book i held in my hands   in the corner of what was once a church
ragged fireweed, blocks & ruin, rain   so it was a different place but still
there remained an inner sanctuary where they knelt, the ones who were left
when the bombs went off   i stood in fireweed out in the sun where day seemed
to have distanced all that   except for the book i picked up   a Common Prayer-
book so fused by fire it had become a box of pages eaten away at the heart —

turning it over there in the back a child's hand transfixed from
wrist to fingertip   strands of charred hand   imprinted by light
across a blackened book

iv

her hands, when i saw her dead, were halfcurled like those of a child asleep

v

hands,   in dream there are hands   of a mother who becomes a child who goes off
into the power hole alone   (& the cry, reiterated, comes from very far, we thought
we heard   a cry   let it be the other side of dreaming, that other being born
into a world made visible

so wipe the table bare, this table where we place our different hands that have not done
with making books or bread or any of the offerings we bring   you wipe the table bare
you wipe it carefully, completely &, in the wetness of wood shining, here is not your
table or our table or their table   here is a table we sit to where our hands rest or move
as the words speak out of their separate quiet   speak of a strangeness our hands
cannot remove.

space activities

black, crow, leap up   fall, flap nervous wings against a steep
invisible   bank, against wind flutter, settle   with none of the
sweep & glide the gulls have   open to this incessant oncoming
tide   waves & foam   wind
                                        crow, rise up &
(drop something   rise & (drop, flutter in to your own stress
landing against this wind, over & over.   cracking shells, having
learned this from the gulls?

                                        through time & a rising
wind last night i dreamt, & see, now, like the crow what it is
i learn from you
                        walking
                                        walking the night as moon
moves out of cancer, moon & sea pre-eminent, walking the long
tiderow beach alone   white shells, white gull-backs on the farther
strand,   lift   into sudden air, clapping wings at re-entry into their
element   birds know wind changes   fast as the moon, how tide
makes sand disappear, no place to be   except the turbulent face of
sea itself incessant

                                        it was you who entered my
dream, entered me   in the rising wind last night, in love, in the wash
of opening seas we come together in   something about a newborn
you saw rise (& drop, rise) & drop   a long life line down through all
these threshing seas, these birds like refugees are resting in *cloud
earth sky sensorium*   outside my dream, outside our particular
"ends & boundaries"   this marvellous Animate we reach, along
with the sweep & glide that gulls possess   this (aery shell) their
& our   one & only   world

where we live

that windowpane fingernail moon last night   coming into the dark
for something outside the bright where i'd left him in the bath having
clipped tiny fingernails all over the blue carpet   all over a blue so black
stars shine   moon mostly a finger of light the crack of a door in the dark
looking back   the encircling a child makes arms around knees in the wet
listening to voices in another room promise tomorrow   a fable   or full
some pencil mark in the nightsky   so faint it is the reverse of night

the other side of where he sits hugging himself in a tepid shoe, a moon
in a funny clog he sails off in, wishing …

a gateway into what remains dark for you, the nave of an abandoned ship
belly of some chromatic whale you've sideslipped. & then you call me on
the phone in full day   lit with the excitement of what used to be a church,
you say, beached in quiet halfway up a hill overlooking the sea   a dream
"reaching 25 feet up" into invisible light   "i've found the place i want to
live in"

                    & does it sleep dark at night on an empty road? & you?
nothing sleeps not even that briar which buds inside you, waiting spell-
bound for a door to open, your door, your hand on it...

pulled two ways, i finish planting beans & marigolds by twilight.   & just
in time. new moon, our neighbour says, been waiting all month for this —
new moon & moon in taurus, figure you can't get more earthy than that.
i put my hand in it, this dark

architecture of gardens, this block whose visible fences hide the invisible
sympathy of seeds & moon   the same you across the sea wake to, walk
in my imagining a white expanse of beach, dark ribs, white canvas whale or
wall, this moon a door we can't afford to look at, opens in reverse onto a
black&white terrain loves also lives inside of, shadowed by a rising earth,
its changes.

saltsprung

        figure in the bluff — body of first tears
turned inward or (night) "wildly gesticulating" — old
man in the burning wood (who are they?) these figures who
come up thru coals, thru night's aging — problematic

smell of kelp, different grasses at night when the dew
starts falling (does it?) this sky lucid as sense &
meaning nothing — twilight — some pink banner trailing
sea darker now, while starting underfoot earth cools & then
our backs — (what figures at?
                    these springs which clarify salt,
sorrow the fluid we rise from

he is young, too young to know, & you are older — i am in-
between — sea darkens around us in the cold suck of time
day forgets as we head (no turning back) into the dark that
cools our ardour — only salt grass on volcanic rock, only
these strange white quartz seams like love or like a fine
desire, like fear all our being frozen in

                            salt-lingering
night, the cooling off of sense — when moon rises incessant insistent
a white nothing on earth generates — no yesterdays within it

one spoonful

> *one does not willingly take the honey*
> Robin Blaser

at the price of sugar we
cannot afford to use
one spoonful extra, one

    "spoonful, spoonful"

honey, to call
you who love sugar
honey, a cinnamon
moth, the poet said
rings in my ear

i cleared the spoons
i cleared a space & a cinnamon
rush flew up in my head his house
full of other things
the moth the lure
thick as honey & furry
under tongue

      (moth wings, moth
      mutter rapid
      against my skin

      a frenzy, this

      is not love which leaves
      its taste on my lips

whatever is wells up like
light this morning after the dark
we all took part in

eating our hearts out
leaving thick rings of desire

web-sticky, we
revel more in the dark
consuming what
declares itself

       (alone, alone i see you
        inconsolable

wrung light thin
as honey thins
in sun

the drop
from love to light

given the right angle
a spoon sheets it

meant

for Roy in La Push

if intent would
give up, let words utter
what they offer
broken in their
rush on

                  us two
                  given to

                  apart

we'd listen to them
break forever
pebbles' crash & pull
our difficult particulars

suspended, each

                  noun
                  awash

a wave collapsed upon

the coast of our
astonishments

listen

he was reading to her, standing on the other side of the kitchen counter where she was making salad for supper, tender orange carrot in hand, almost transparent at its tip, slender, & she was wondering where such carrots came from in winter. he was standing in the light reading to her from a book he was holding, her son behind him at the table where amber light streamed from under a glass shade she had bought for its warm colour midwinter, though he had called it a cheap imitation of the real thing.

in its glow her son was drawing red Flash & blue Superman into a comic he was making, painstakingly having stapled the pages together & now with his small & definite hand trying to draw exact images of DC Superstars & Marvel heroes none of them had ever seen except in coloured ink.

but he was reading to her about loss, excited, because someone had named it at last, was naming even as he read, the shape of what he felt to be his own, recognized at last in words coming through him from the page, coming to her through his emphatic & stirred voice stumbling over the rough edges of terms that weren't his, even as he embraced them. lost, how their dancing had lost touch with the ring dance which was a collective celebration, he said.

she was standing with the grater in one hand, carrot in the other, wondering if the grating sound would disturb him. she wanted to hear what had stirred him. she wanted to continue the movement of making salad which, in the light & the löwenbrau they shared, was for once coming so easily, almost was spring stirring around the corner of the house in a rhythm of rain outside she was moving in, had moved, barely knowing it was rain beyond the wetness of walking home —

hand in hand, he was saying, a great circle like the circle of the seasons, & now people barely touch, where at least with the waltz they used to dance in couples, then with rock apart but *to* each other, whereas now, he caught her eye, the dances we've been to you can see people dancing alone, completely alone with the sound.

lifting the carrot to the grater, pressing down, watching flakes of orange fall to the board, she felt accused in some obscure way, wanted to object (it was her generation after all), thought up an obscure argument about how quadrilles could be called collective in ballrooms where privileged guests took their assigned places in the dance. but now, & she recalled the new year's eve party they'd been to, almost a hundred people, strangers, come together, & people don't know each other in the city the way they used to in a village. but that only glanced off what the book was saying about husbandry & caring for the soil as a collective endeavour.

the whole carrot was shrinking into a thousand flakes heaped & scattered at once, the whole carrot with its almost transparent sides shining in the light, had ground down to a stump her fingers clutched close to the jagged pockets of tin that scraped them, she saw her fingers, saw blood flying like carrot flakes, wondered why she imagined blood as part of the salad …

listen, he was saying, this is where he's really got it. & he read a long passage about their imprisonment in marriage, all the married ones with that impossible ideal of confining love to one — *one cannot love a particular woman unless one loves womankind,* he read. listen, he said, & he read her the passage about the ring dance, about the participation of couples in one great celebration, the *amorous feast that joins them to all living things.* he means fertility, she said, thinking, oh no, oh back to that, woman's one true function. he means the fertility of the earth, he said, he means our lives aware of seasonal growth & drawing nourishment from that instead of material acquisition & exploitation. listen, he read a passage about sexual capitalism, about the crazy images of romance that fill people's heads, sexual freedom & skill & the me-generation on all the racks of all the supermarket stores.

using her palms like two halves of a split spoon, she scooped up the heap of carrot flakes & dropped them onto a plate of lettuce, dark because it was romaine torn into pieces in the wooden bowl with other green things. dance. in & out. she watched the orange flakes glisten in their oil of skin, touch the surfaces of green she tossed with real spoons, each flake dipping into the dark that lay at the heart of, what, *their* hearts, as they had, the other night, sunk into bed at the end of the party, drunk & floating, their laughter sifting in memory through conversations, wrapt in the warmth of what everyone had said & how they had moved away & toward each other & loved in very obscure ways, slowly they had made love to everyone they loved in each other, falling through & away from their separate bodies — listen, she said, as the rain came up & she set the salad on the wooden table underneath the lamp.

a series of takes

> *Because speech is not a weapon. It's a place.*
> Marguerite Duras

it's rain repeating us, not anything light, shining half-day bursts through cloud cover, all my raspberries tight-green dwarfs. as if we wade in suspense, not towards summer but away from ourselves. similar. even the lawn wet & the cat's mud paw fishing through slats for mud hands planting would-be flowers. comparative. everything swims similitudes of flourishing — the too-green light of elsewhere, fancying what or who?

. . . .

rain repeats. we'd gone fishing for change. heads it was Pasolini, his Boccaccio tableaux illumined by the story-teller's fancy, wilful even as those gods in their carefully structured garden gave him sight, a blow across the eyes like retribution likes. he fancied (torture in that caress an incandescent fact), fancied himself a lover

contemporary in this, liking the limelight, inserting himself as author into what he makes, or who ...

came forward to greet us on the brink of a greek terrazzo after words, another set of similitudes, *my friends!* we barely know this angel with the ingrown eyes grown loud downing brandy after brandy, off to the Bahamas, money in his hands & poems in the offing. such high stakes. *i'll get him, i can write circles around him,* infernal still at the centre of his doubt, who took him for love & found love's rivalry a hell

Pasolini was good in '74. in these circles of better, best. repeating the same frame. reversing their roles (who screwed who). writing circles around the divine still blazing up in his mind. *i'll get him* he says. *you'll see.*

. . . .

see rain repeating rains desire in a retinal caress, as if muscular, as of some inner eye a flickering set of images will give. *in the early morning when your eyelids flicker i know you're watching your own movie* you say. & whose film do you fancy then?

caught in the visible, everything swims in parallel. & out of touch (this green light go-ahead, this gel that holds us in suspense & separate). we could see ourselves in a serial light, a series of other takes. deep below dream & given to nothing but place.

retrieving madrone

take, take the

        arbutus, crazy-woman tree, she said, does
everything at the wrong time, sheds last years' leaves mid-
summer, yellow, out of new green, sheds ochre bark at the
end of summer when

        you'd think she'd hang onto it

                        the way
light catches in the curled edges of her

                    skin, it's only
paper, thin enough to let light, as the words of this world
impinge, turn me out of mine. i throw off words, leave out-
grown images of myself

        crazy-waving-in-air ma-
drone this murmur you make, a stir of bright
leaves hitting home, the sound of *geta*, his
name for the thongs he wears against sharp
things on his path underfoot: a name, a use

overhead, over my head, i listen to slippery
woman, word peeler, leaf weaver, hear the slur
of a different being approach

        leaf   lingua   love-
              tongue
                turning me
inside out

the tri-cornered heart

attract: asparagus fern by our bed, its one wood cherry clinging, will,
long after the fragrant flowers are gone, hang on, still drawn to what?
i'm drawn, & not to clinging.

it's not a frailty of will, yours & the drunks on Powell — hapless you
said, helpless you meant, vagrant. it's when the rains come not to water
flowers (they do) but drizzle in your eye the misery of self gone vacant,

torn between. two yous. to you & you, from the used heart, the over-
exposed, petals fallen.

bring me in out of the rain this perfect yellow tulip opening in the warmth
of kitchen (irresistible) to full, spread, glory of lemon (ha, quick intake of
breath astonished *hh* in the heart of, lemon) smudges at the base of what
you call this tri-cornered heart, green, this stark geometry.

hearth with the missing *h* of heart, sound shifter. earth & a breath released.

how our two-way streets transform overnight traffic flows one way in an
attempt to unblock the heart. congestion. volleying. cars desires ride,
images in our eyes. will make us want — what?
want.

to want the moon: that abstract rock.

a note said your studio had been broken into & when i phoned you said a
drunk had fallen through. shards of glass & blood. fallen into an empty
lens where no photograph exists. he wasn't aware of risk, he went away
in a city ambulance & now there is a hole where he was.

a hole in the heart where love sounds its breath out into what is.

the eye & the heart. slightly crazy in their synapse. crazy walking down
town last night, down the welfare street of disembodied strangers reeling
under a moon dematerialized, violent & pissing in desperate reassurance of
the familiar. sirens go all night. the sirens in our head all right. fences &
windows blowing with the cold, gone open, gone naked, stepping slowly
through a hole in a plateglass window, snatching the biggest fish to cradle
(blue lips again). gone empty. gone mirror. gone looking thanks.

want hurts, want implies a lack in what has been. the avocado wants water.
& light. & earth. each day all over again.

we want it simple: all the ways we lean on each other, love to be counted on
as home, that place we belong. turn off the light & lock the door. while the
world grows wild outside, the other face of desire (turn, turn to the moon), a
complex paranoia breeds radioactive flowers, bread lines the poor "deserve,"
a climb in numbers that bleed "us" white

versions of the inconsolable, uncontainable. in the spread of our being here
in the flesh. flawed.

the tulip's petal skins fell silvery & awry in the sink, at sixes & …
baring a triangular heart, greener now & nude, exudes one clear drop, one
tiny bleeding sound.

eart. second person singular between the sound of heart, the sound of
hearth. me in you. & you.

people are not flowers, last longer, die longing. for what's wanted leans
visibly like a flower or a lemon tree over the fence.

origin obscure, & why ask? *līmūn.* not something eggshaped & yellow, thing
to hold. no thing but a ringing sound, a taste we move in, drawn in wild flows,
wild (yellow) flowers outward in that moment

juice:

let me take you apart, you said. the room dark, radio silent in the green heart
of something new & known.

life expectancy

pok   pok   pok   pok   water drops   measurable time mocks
a form of water torture   mis/translated   mist   "heavy water"
missed   knowing what they do to us   in the dusk   the blue
cooling towers of Three Mile Island   blue reactors they
don't know what to do with   elements glowing

                                                  in this bath
under the eaves of our mutable house   a child revels   sky dark blue
at ten   going on june   this amber hold on time   fools us
our lives sleeping   spent

                        too much missed reason   too little
long view   *deuterium used as moderator & coolant*   heavy water
used fuel elements   with nowhere to go   glow blue radio-
active for *300,000 years   crowded into temporary holding pools*
this build-up   mist in the mirror   time   this terror

power they want   a fix on   the earth   it costs us

water to water calls   water to earth   seeks its own level
nothing puts it out this blue   water glow   weird &
beautiful our children   practicing death in their cells

                                            outside
killdeer skim the ghost of False Creek waters   drained & recon-
structed   skim the playground pool the drinking fountain plays
alone in the dark to no one *killee   kill   dee*

                                                    you hear? you
here? slightly blue as i call   as you answer water   soaks in our
sleeping ears   fear is the fuel we inhale   that drugged sense of
nothing to be done   no air to breathe play   fools the present
currents we live within   invisible rivers these birds wing
breath & solar wind   or else this blue
mist the distance we
fail to reach
through

.

seeing it go up in smoke

"as if"
what happens is only the flare of a cigarette. he is smoking. she is watching
summer and smoke. they have driven through the valley in a haze of summer
sharing the silence of twilight. the silence is sharing, or. silence is a screen
between them, silence reflects what does not get said. the apparent silence
of two heads looking, each inside its own space

"as if nothing"
were happening he said, gesturing toward the light his camera shares, performance
intent, having brought the mask that makes his face an inner room. they had
rented the room, had viewed it, viewed the bed and tv screen she had already
foreseen, taking his mask which is an image of himself as the outer face of a movie
she is trying to silence in her head. the way words keep moving in their supposing.
what might he make of it (what he has seen) and has she seen behind (a screen) his
image of it?

"nothing untoward"
he means toward her he does not reveal intent but lets it, whatever that is, happen.
as it happens her listening to, but she is also watching, the talkies he once said she
is given to, given over completely he means, taken over by, this incessant ripple of
motive: will she? does he? have something else in mind? stretched out on the bed
she is intent on following the reach of their desire. does he think she wants to fill
up the silence between? or does she think smokescreen, seeing him compose in
silent frames that other movie he is making, the tv screen a part of what he com-
poses, his nudity opposes (it, her, them). speaking thus to her, or speaking to his
camera? like summer's going up

"were"

he says toward their watching where they are going, don't mind me, meaning (a)side or (un)toward meaning nothing is happening but him (nude) and her (fully clothed) watching him masked, or the mask and him, take place elsewhere she has fallen between. she is not there where he is watching himself watch her watching summer smoke in some imagined south they have not entered where, behind the mask and silently, desire is to be viewed

"happening"

between and out of it she feels is it but it is, the camera making it happen. pull the plunger will you, he says, in the blink of an eye that takes her where he has posed himself at the edge of her attention. is he the movie then? he is the making and making it opposes her viewing what is made, though in seeing it she is re-making a movie that goes on viewing itself in the smoke of being unseen "as if nothing untoward were happening"

new year / new where

pot earth   under a fingernail   comes alive (smells   only when
wet)   somehow ferns survive   dry   our forgetful hello/goodbye
driving habitual roads last night   arrival calls   under the bridge how
roads converge   the bridge is all approach & curves   into memory's
late-night daughter who arrives as we smell earth rise up in winter's
pre-spring warmup

                she so much your daughter, quick to leap
black hat with feather (grouse?)   with the quickness of flight for somewhere
else

                drawn to a litany of arrival we follow
the road under granville street bridge   "island" quiet now   tracing our
curve in the dark these struts support   this bridge-approach & turn
left then right to cobble end   old trolley-train track & wall of brick
blind   corner   past molson's parking lot the plant itself
burrard   this pall   all fiery   dust   the traffic raises
fast & gone

          on edge   on the edge of departure innocent
of roads to take   she thrums up anyhow   out of old grief's familial
bush she wants to beat   about those roots on other ground   we urge
keep us in touch   with how life there   curves into you

                  how right
at breakfast it occurred   to start the year in february when life   its ghost
begins to rise up into these matted & winter-saturated stems   leaves   even
those indoors recessed into themselves   in want, in want   what can any
one provide?

she flies off just as the year begins   & we lose sight of what
makes us come alive   this curve of tensile points   this drive under the
bridge supports   their strut & arc   the road we use to get home turns
at a blind corner

— *sleeping the sleep of the worn* —

while unseen leaves illumine moon   a ceiling starred   even under the pall
of traffic we wake to place & then it fades   stretching new fronds into day
hair down   brushing it out in the open air   sprung, Jan, you've flown
your coop   here's to arrival some new where

HERE & THERE

(1980-2000)

arriving

i arrive depleted, cramped from the embrace of space rushing
forward to meet it is. driving very close to flying, not, after all,
arms afloat but rushing in air, a grip on the wheel flashing lights
when the oncoming overtaker won't give way & afterwards the
impossibly possible replay. flight. over the edge of every barrier
meant to prevent such launching into open space, car flipping over
in a barrage of trees of scree of flame ...

those curved hindrances to flying off the road, concrete barricade
(once earth-filled barrels) set to keep your feet on, in this case, wheels.
as wheels perhaps made those breaks in the asphalt painted white as in
gone-over, or yellow colour of warning (keep-to-your-side), those black
bituminous falls, whole side of a hill slipping in miniature. whole side
of a mountain dropped on the Hope-Princeton ...

but the onrunning ongoing something to do with the way people
passing your camera enter incessant muybridge shifts through
aperture repeat (glasses still on a moving dash still trees seem to
rush up against) you there in your studio bent over a photo grid
eyes tracing the movement from frame to frame

& i have not arrived until i can write how arms of the peopled earth
push into the river to land. & landed here, am bushed. while air still
rushes away trees stand all over the ridge of these mountains untouched
by volcanic ash she said in Osoyoos had ambushed her roses

sun drops early here the valley so narrow night thick with a ground
swell of vegetation dew or spittle of insects' thrilling their being
constantly declared beyond borders, wet seeps rousing earth to
excel, exceed its turning all these small voices over to the limit of
mountains

& even the mountains under cover of dark run on, range after effortless
range, dreaming they run on running, earth running fire, running
to arrive

.

where

for David McFadden

where we were we had come to in time, faces craning up at
wild/ blue/ over there, over the brow of the mountain they
are coming (sky), out of the eye of that cloud (divers). daddy,
a child cried, i don't feel well. don't stare at the sun, his father
advised.

we're sitting bareheaded on hot cement, an old breakwater affair.
& when did you last have an affair with a breakwater he jokes broken
hearted. it only hurts when i'm here. he means when she's here in his
head. it hurts for those who do not mind their hearts, that chakra he is
learning to open where mind is.

he means she is not here where he is, on the shore of a lake no bigger
than a river & so close to the mountain they would appear from (sky-
leapers), the crest of, the other side of another valley away

another state another notion away in the desert where had they
got to? bodies of 9 women & 2 men curled around bodies of
cactus in smaller bodies of shade. they fought, the survivors said,
for drops of piss to wipe their faces, wet their lips, yellow water
leaked by each body fighting to keep its bitter stink of want here,
crossing the border in secret, wanting to reach LA in high heels of
anticipation, wanting to get there when here is insupportable.

a breakwater he said, needing a border, a barricade against high
tides of emptiness. this empty mountain air. this sun emptying
in its radiance. reduces each body, burning off the fat, burning off
the pale moon of idea.

you'll see, he said. but we hadn't come for this empty circle of sand
ringed with anticipation. we had come for the lama — gone for a hike
up the mountain his door said. everywhere he goes he is followed by
14 hungry ghosts. & can he feed them?

so leaving the 7 offering bowls of yellow water strewn with crimson,
the fallen petals of roses, of generation, sutras, steps along
the way. leaving the red & yellow columbines by the door of Tashi
Choling, we slipped through a hole in the fence into their waiting

here a child is burning up, here bodies are falling. out of a blue sky
they come twirling small pavilions of red, of white, they come leaping
nylon suits down drafts of air, pumping, pulling all their strings through
the narrow valley they manoeuver to land. & folding up their parachutes
they are gone.

inside

for Zasep Tulku Rinpoche

inside a room near Lakeside Park (not the lake, she says, it's where
the west arm of the lake lets out its river), inside a room close with
heat that rain outside has driven off to mountain ridges where it
sparks in odd & brilliant flashes, in still dusk people crowd 3 of
the room's walls. in front of the 4th, window closed against gathering
night, he sits by a low table. lightning plays over his shoulder, pink
if you don't look quick enough, blue, to catch its colour.

Awakened Mind, he offers, what is that? just as a flash of lightning
outlines the contours of land the sentence he sends his Tibetan
English through, quick as high tension electrical discharge shifts in
a flash from *me* to *you*

we drop our eyes, gaze inward as rapid chatter hurries parking
meters through mind's space, sheet lightning the underside of
disparate foci. thoughtcloud surge & batter. fenderbender
bounce off any shiny me & mine.

out the corner of an eye he wears saffron, sits bare arms at rest
in the hungry thought-crowd of our restlessness, unknown, what
thoughts flare through his mind. a bowl of saffron water stilled in
its self-offering —

when she asks are you really a Bodhisattva? a chuckle rips up from
his belly, something that tickles the inside of his mind & chuckling
ripples out to us: i don't know, i am checking.

to begin with

begin with a, you write, & written over *a, i.* begin with *i* on the
back of the envelope in which you mail your greeting to me, sound
of the river of your playing, thrum of the zither, rush of white
water, & the ticking of your watch. "turn it on," you write, listen
to the hum of an electric typewriter metering time's throb & strum,
of blood in your wrist, in your tongue: "this is the song the mighty
Skeena taught."

this is the song the Kootenay teaches as i ride its turns, its dammed
up falls of metered water measured in a hum of wires mounting
green tree swathes of mountain ranges, metric, those wires run over
mountain miles to end in the coast's big city flare of electric shine.

yet river runs, over its dam it keeps on coming, small trickles, tiny
diversions round that wall of concrete curbing its blue welling ...

i don't know what i want. want keeps running ahead to be here
where nothing is wanting but you. who do not want. who does
not want? i make you *he*, object out there so seeing you i can be
clear. of want? you are not here. you want for nothing. nothing lives
in a full house where even silence runs, ticking, metering what is left.
nothing is left but you & you are in the midst of hearing, seeing, &
savouring it fully.

leaving me with me crossing *a*   (gap)   i string out bridges of words
to seek you there. between us the rushing abyss, a not, undone. undoing
all my bridges in a blue so clear you & i fade to a single note impossible
to sound.

proximity

held in, held breath explodes gargoyle cheeks full of hotspring
water, smacked, issue a delighted stream/scream, out of the way
of Rinpoche cavorting with his brother-student-friend, porpoise
sendup ripples in their wake leaping, both of them, under & up
into air (it rained) ringed by cedar by swallow skim.

lake out there, & a world scarcely shipshape. eye drops held space
for the immediate, girls with hairdos frantic to escape & middleaged
scowlers muttering russian retreat. all action speech, all speech held
in pool's effusive steam released to a cool trees aspire to, horizonless
air.

hh   huh   ha   his release the measure of contained hours spent
sitting from 4 years on recognized as returned incarnate once again
to teach. that impossibly possible repeat.

springs up from earth's heart, he says. yes, but how? & waves us in
to a cave hotter & lowtunnelled, stooped inside a passageway a spray
hot mineral water down walls mucous-smooth & slippery we slide in
deeper, held — no face no name no breath no space no up nor down
nor out

                    (have to

explode where sky is, her face lifted to the moon wears a wan smile,
selene sinking all of her into the warmth of waters gone contained with
difference: here swallows skim the surface, feet touch ground, multiple
bathers constrained, particular selves joined in one warmth below, cool
separateness above —

face it, we are separate & contained. some sorrow in us like distance
waiting for wings to pierce it.

released, they are hollering animal howls in the back cavern of earth
echoing osprey, bull moose, wordless. imagine mountain giving birth
to speech? imagine! she sinks smiling into water, language our horizon
(o breath) limit.

here

is afloat, & cold & moon lights the whole of sky above, lakeface
below. somewhere a beaver is swimming 60 pounds of oily fur
submerged. somewhere fish are skimming the underside of legs
& logs, whole auras bristling through water

are you coming? i call. to whom? two stand on shore, hard-to-see
bodies wheeling a single flashlight distance erases, no path across,
just flicker writing the dark there where they are.

here i am i cry to the big dipper wheeling so slow overhead no
one sees it go by. here i am, osprey cries, black wingspread
skimming our heads in dark water. darker logs. white points
of stars, *sitareh*, elsewhere flashing into our sky

we occur in a splash, a rush into black. we occur between this
murky bottom & the arched & starred vault of heaven, no camber,
no curve or curb now, this chamber roofless floats off into space.
heaven is where we occur.

one in the water catches up & we swim to a log that smells of tree
skin. imagine beaver allure, living your days in the smell of wet
wood, wet fur twisting & diving into the heart of tree remains.

ah, romance, he says. & vivid on the hill, dogs, inchoate, inarticulate,
or not in words anyhow, hurl their longing at the moon so full of
herself. romance, he says, hit me hard. i wasn't prepared, considering —

a wailing sound, bends round the track in advance of itself, this rival
light a late-night freight bewails its coming. in its flare we tread water,
watch its rolling roar of white illumine just one side of cottonwoods noon

afloat on shiny water trying to explain — there weren't many trains
on my track. as it fades, as it rolls on into no one's black heaven.

from somewhere

from somewhere downhill trumpet notes rise on the rustling air,
up, in the scale of a story. river rushes out of view around the
bend, through the corner of an eye, not ever leaving.

proceeding is how we think we go on, the increasing current of
water's push off/ push away from, limits (instant definition of
a riverbank) —

then what keeps this wasp returning & returning to my hand's
sweat here, some other type of meat? my yellow top some other
flower? what draws us back? what moves us to repeat?

desire the allure, the shine we are caught by. every longing an attempt
on the stars.

not the whole story. crows in an uproar scare off the curious osprey.
i scare her off her nest by swimming below, lured by the way she banks,
she soars, tail feathers spread, screaming alarm at my insistent, my
circling head

this desire for connection as large as the lines that connect starshine.

while solitary, plaintive, heart sound rises from the lake, a recognizable
refrain some boat circling takes us through, a transient air mountains
share, even as the current carries trumpeter, heart & music out of view.

SMALL PRINT

for Betsy

small print

i

how little the reach, what is *love* love? its
impossible repeat attenuated through telephone
wire the light letter language of 'fax it,' hearts
darling and x's intend body's imprint, stand in for
the unremitting smell of your skin just there at
neck's bony hollow in your hair both kinds that
arc the pelvic ridge keys your other speech
close up and swollen lips aflare with wet
declaration *bold face* — without which i sleep
small print in the white of the page

ii

print small print it small enough not
to reach all of what love says when it
reads small in the whole of the page

iii

reading your voice attentive to solitude a
transient space love infiltrates anticipates
the feel of your skin its smell no word (nearness
then) resplendent breasting under the covers a
breathing space the city occludes its neon news
your voice removed my body walks its carbon
copy of yours deep in the bone

iv

not ready for you to say not ready print
not love printout plain as day not
ready you say for me to come home

v

to reach those little loves the pain of hills
animal words love-stark, enter in white a
void of cross-hatching covering distance unknown
intent scrawls xmas drift along the creek i follow
your declarative slant as you ascend out of the
limits of love a joy you wished language written
in quick gesture bold stride new reference i
try to decipher

vi

last call (it) how fast we unravel
love calls us i recall it
beside ourselves

vii

it's hearts darling attentive through tension to
the wire that closes round them stripping each
remark that separates familiar connection future
version sprung as nearness cuts with a ping the
words impossible and audible attachment taut to
the breaking point's heart strung

viii

love won't compute can't connect
words with what's felt, the fragile
murmur of memory fade, Y *save?*

ix

these small paraphs we sign trying the hours to
separate what's yours from mine, stand-in for
tongue's unremitted (f)lick keying the whole body
now no longer sent dot matrix gone to cruise two
truths *u* and *i* resolve out through, shaky vowels
looking for consonance where static interrupts
a clutch of mismatched lines. stop. no line at

x

repeat it small repeat all of
what love calls us back to

xi

night's byline grief enters quick mis/
take halfasleep makes the weight of the cat
curled in my groin your curve my hollow intimates
instant line of hip hand follows through on
empty, *you your* erased from day's vocabulary

xii

turned out of the inmost
intimate, cord between

/cut/

your body and the word

xiii

leaves with this scrawl all of it unread
silence cannot cure septic override snow's late
light intensifies abstraction now skin's kinetics
fade i'm left disfiguring you

breakup inters trust
the dream *we*
entered in

        imagination's scrap

SEA SHINING BETWEEN

"Mytilène, parure et splendeur de la mer"
Renée Vivien

"… the island of women as a central
mind in a culture sank like Atlantis
and went out of history"
Judy Grahn

booking passage

You know the place: then
Leave Crete and come to us
Sappho/Mary Barnard

this coming & going in the dark of early morning, snow scribbling its thaw-line round the house. we are under-cover, under a cover of white you unlock your door on this slipperiness.

to throw it off, this cover, this blank that halts a kiss on the open road. i kiss you anyway, & feel you veer toward me, red tail lights aflare at certain patches, certain turns my tongue takes, provocative.

we haven't even begun to write... sliding the in-between as the ferry slips its shore-line, barely noticeable at first, a gathering beat of engines in reverse, the shudder of the turn to make that long passage out —

the price paid for this.

we stood on the road in the dark. you closed the door so carlight wouldn't shine on us. our kiss reflected in snow, the name for this.

under the covers, morning, you take my scent, writing me into your cells' history. deep in our sentencing, i smell you home.

there is the passage. there is the booking — & our fear of this.

you, sliding past the seals inert on the log boom. you slide & they don't raise their heads. you are into our current now of going, not inert, not even gone as i lick you loose. there is a light beginning over the ridge of my closed eyes.

passage booked. i see you by the window shore slips by, you reading Venice our history is, that sinking feel, those footings under water. i nose the book aside & pull you forward gently with my lips.

a path, channel or duct. a corridor. a book & not a book. not booked but off the record. this.

irresistible melt of hot flesh. furline & thawline align your long wet descent.

nothing in the book says where we might head. my tongue in you, your body cresting now around, around this tip's lip- suck   surge   rush of your coming in other words.

we haven't even begun to write ... what keeps us going, this rush of wingspread, this under (nosing in), this wine-dark blood flower. this rubbing between the word and our skin.

*   *   *

"tell me, tell me where you are" when the bush closes in, all heat a luxuriance of earth so heavy i can't breathe the stifling wall of prickly rose, skreek of mosquito poised ... for the wall to break

the wall that isolates, that i so late to this: it doesn't, it slides apart — footings, walls, galleries, this island architecture

one layer under the other, memory a ghost, a guide, histolytic where the pain is stored, murmur, mer-*mère*, historicity stored in the tissue, text ... a small boat, fraught. trying to cross distance, trying to find that passage (secret) in libraries where whole texts, whole persons have been secreted away.

original sin he said was a late overlay. & under that & under that? sweat pouring down, rivers of thyme and tuberose in the words that climb toward your scanning eyes

She shouts aloud, Come! we know it;
thousand-eared night repeats that cry
across the sea shining between us

*   *   *

this tracking back & forth across the white, this tearing of papyrus crosswise, this tearing of love in our mouths to leave our mark in the midst of rumour, coming out.

… to write in lesbian.

the dark swell of a sea that separates & beats against our joined feet, islands me in the night, fear & rage the isolate talking in my head. to combat this slipping away, of me, of you, the steps … what was it we held in trust, tiny as a Venetian bead, fragile as words encrusted with pearl, *mathetriai*, not-mother, hidden mentor, lost link?

to feel our age we stood in the road in the dark, we stood in the roads & it was this old, a ripple of water against the hull, a coming and going

we began with …

her drowned thyme and clover, fields of it heavy with dew our feet soak up, illicit hands cupped one in the other as carlights pick us out. the yell a salute. marked, we are elsewhere, translated here ...

like her, precisely on this page, this mark: *a thin flame runs under / my skin.*
twenty-five hundred years ago, this trembling then. actual as that which wets
our skin her words come down to us, a rush, poured through the blood, this
coming & going among islands is.

central to the periphery

what if the islands are lost? what if the waters
cover the Hesperides? they would rather remember —
                                        H.D.

on the periphery of vision small waves enter your eye successively fluent
laps running in from the outer edge murmuring news of horizon, that bound
and beneficence,

         … as if the island of your eye were central & wave-breaking
wealth dawned from the sea beyond we are small, a part of

cold on the periphery of our kiss, a chill wind brings news of ocean going dead,
of fishing down the food web harvesting smaller & smaller life now cod, haddock,
skate have disappeared, daily this list of what is dropping away

news-breaking waves, & not peripheral your eye mirrors a last windsail jittering
pink & declarative the banners we used to fly flaming our kiss above stranded kelp

brilliant, daughters of Hesperus we thought we glimpsed Paradise on the edge of
our shared vision
                as if without pupil
                or all pupil, dark
                yet very clear with amber
                shining

small messages erased, & left again to be erased, your legible eye holds mine, a current steady & inviolate between us, night & the first stars coming on

feet beyond our feet, subsurface plankton generating half the oxygen we breathe fade into an engineered night outlasting more than dawn's fine-mesh trawls that stripmine ocean floor

peripheral to my sight of you, peripheral yet superimposed, these white telegrams of death delivered into your eye not even love can erase their foam letters whispering continuity gone, heuristic, earth & all that surrounds us charged with alteration, even that making well which would circle and set us intricate in place here on the edge

out of the pallor of your face afloat on darkening sand you look right through an old horizon, that world-crack, that margin of plenty … on & on we are learning how far we extend

the approach re-approached by ferry

rounding the point engines slow i go

out in wood smell up close home in house-lit twilight's intimate
would-reach, could-touch

                        this celebrated air, imagine

nearness in your hand on the glass that separates, inside looking
out

                    (green awake that slows arrival there)

or outside reading in: you in the lounge illumined, strange, i want
not to frame, your hair whose scent its very nearness then

Nearness so pronounced ... it makes all discrimination of identity

into the kiss that blurs outside/in quick tongue's intent

and thus

                    green dream recedes at the shore

all forms of property, impossible

"you" no different, no other than co-terminous with air, the light
shrill, cicada-like

                    home dream in our hands let go, let go

the shape that grief takes

> *One island*
> *bleeding into the next*
>   Rachel Rose

when it breaks, lifting not belly but ceiling, low cloud cover shedding immaculate islands light-edged & drifting

                        archipelago, that first sea mirrors sky, island studded or scattered it mirrors our West Coast Aegean, a series of rocky droplets — the bleeding memory does as it tries to patch over a sudden gulf

curious ellipsis of rock, this falling short, each one alone in what can't be said, we ferry across, jaunting from port to port, unable to see fear deepening between

us as we were, on one of those fragrant isles, thyme covered, honey suckled drowse, some sheltered patch between rocks in a wind that stormed for days & all the power cut. Hotel Sapfo a week ahead of season, *don't worry about Visa,* Aeolia bored with marriage in wine-coloured jeans twisting a strand of long black curly hair while Mama scours out the kitchen

                through half-closed doors sea brilliant, restless, agitated smile that silhouettes these rocky spots we dally for a while
.

shutters banging, promenade trees springy & wild. we were one of those freighters swinging at anchor. we were windblown chamomile & crimson poppy. we were oddly triangular navigators of thunderous currents for honey, sensing our way back to Sapphic *abrosuma, a delicate sumptuousness [to be] accurately enjoyed.*

but then, the long soughing out & out of surf as it concatenated water on pebbles repeated all along the shore, insistent breakage heard only as rhythm, pages turning in an unlit shop, the archaic smile of Kore leapt up satisfied, replete, that seashore smile of a people close to distance & light, able to hold the in-between in their sun-dazzled gaze

                          gone blind, you said, pointing out

no pupil

& thence to Nice, La Perouse tucking its white walls against *le rocher*, its shifting-level surprise terraces dreaming a way to intimacy, we slept, sipped a last coffee in our room before you left for Amsterdam & i for home, delayed, wandering a floor bright with distance

separated from Sappho by much more than   sea & sundazzle   islands drifting further & further away

crossing

small lights in the dark coming up across water, arc

out of wind rush, transient, intransigent beating forward to reach
(you) bridge (that gap) your leaving left caressed skin baffled
in nowhere-space

still, deck underfoot's some footing, rail cupped in a palm's solid
let's say, contained

     L'art du toucher, complexe et curieux ... Renée notes

but it's not you i touch, am touched by — you mislaid in memory's
ache for what — substantial? weight of a thigh, say, yours or mine

longdead fingers, clever lingerers at love's shudder, how desire writes
the ex-lover raking the roots of air, anguish netted there in the mind's
traffic under skin, thin tattoo i strain to read you in

     Ta forme est un éclair qui laisse les bras vides

so arc, so intent that will not cease its beating forward, thrown
(the shudder of the poem's engine in reverse)

     ... *traitress tide*, she epitomizes, *stealing away*

your water mark still legible there in fading skin

passage between

*... quand les questions se succèdent comme
des archipels de sens.*
                                        Nicole Brossard

leap, she said, from one shoreline to the next. in this coming & going
distance illuminates the salt sheen of grief for what was, even moon's
ever-ecstatic silverleaf cresting ferry's wake as onshore lights diminish.
look back, the last dark deck of going's nearly empty, car packed to the
roof & stationary above the throb & grind of an archaic engine, no one
else on deck. i have the whole flatbed of the past to myself, arms out-
stretched & wavering.

leap, she said. description leaks an ache. so turn to the wind, lean
into it over the rail to look at what looms, foam curling away & the
dark shapes of other mountains, light clusters spread, this chain of
attempted footholds in a shifting sea of emptiness.

can the heart's bruise dissipate? closed auricles open in the glow of
pain-wise eyes? yours, laughter-lined & equally hurt.

to leap is to bite into risk, rise to it, breaking the surface of common
sense. what swims below the curl of best intention? what dark shapes
keel a ferry's passage? your wake-ghosts & mine, their reach as yet
indeterminate.

the bruised heart swerves, alive to alternate routes, warm drift-sense.
your smile when light seeps in, the very shift & change of seabed.

to leap, you said, is to land in some new place. same old footing?
how sidestep mind's inscription of itself as this & this me drenched
in its own history, this you unknown & isolate?

what's surface? what depth? in the eruption of circumstance, ancient
ice-free coves for migrants down this coast, slide under. clam-strewn
refugia, stone points: all such markers underwater.

heading south & west, light rimming mountains blind at base, the dark
heart swells. migrant passages of one life through the years converge
on x, tincture of self a light stain sea reflects, humming & heaving toward
an unfamiliar shore that breaks its passage for some place to be.

in the current

                    ... one discovers the immense landscape ... of the passage.
                                                        Hélène Cixous

isle isolé,
            pain enislanded,
                        i stand at your door, quick with your here, my coming

pleasure on the rein leaps with anticipation, pleasure & grief so wound together

It is the passage that can appear ...

with anticipation of your opening, your light step to the door & the landscape that
unfolds its coastal curves, its rocks non-negotiable, its sudden isthmus isthmus oh
hello
        is most fragile for the mouth that connects

                        ... that can appear most difficult.

i'm island, o stranded isolate that hesitates once more at a singular mountain (omitting
mountains' joint footing underwater, o joined jouissant, the world is round she sang)

at your door the body in its forward motion trembles, *trans*-lated is(o *les oiseaux
volants*

at your door — you open it, light flares in a great wedge from beyond your shoulders

                It happens in a flash. In a leap. Without transition ...

welcome streaming out of your eyes. & risk. all the bodies we have loved pass their shadows in transit between us

                                        on the buoyant, in the current of a passage

impossible & yes, in trust

(is love enough?)

Salt through the earth conduct the sea
Olga Broumas

such green glistening, a sparrow preening a far-stretched wing, light full of pleasure-chirping, feathered bodies at home in earth's soft voltage & newness written over your face waking from dream, each blade, each leaf encased still in the wet from last night's rain

is love enough when the breast milk a mother jets in the urgent mouth of her baby is laced with PCBs?

hungry you said, for love, for light, armfulls of daffodils we refuse to gather standing luminous, pale ears listening, ochre trumpets at the heart darkness pools, & the radio, as we sit on a paint-blistered deck in brilliant sun reports that snow, whiter than chalk on the highest shelf of the Rockies is sedimented with toxins

the dead, the dying — we imprint our presence everywhere on every wall & rock

& what is love in the face of such loss?

once dawn, *standing by my bed*, she wrote, *in gold sandals ... that very/ moment* half-awake in a whisper of light her upturned face given to presence, a woman involved, a circle of women she taught how to love, how to pay a fine attention praising simply & correctly the fleeting phases of what is, arrives

we get these glimpses, you said, grizzlies begging at human doorways, two cubs
& a mother so thin her ribs showed prominent under ratty fur, shot now that our
salmon rivers run empty, rivers that were never ours to begin with —

& the sea, the sea goes out a long way in its unpublished killing ground

this webwork — what we don't know about the body, what we don't know may
well be killing us — well : spring : stream : river, these powerful points you set
your fingers on, drawing current through blockages, moving inward, not out, to
see

chi equally in
the salt sea and fields thick with bloom
inner channels & rivers

a sea full of apparent islands, no jetting-off point, no airborne leap possible

without the body all these bodies
interlaced

IMPOSSIBLE PORTRAITURE

for Bridget

impossible portraiture

this way

        elements of a face

                compose themselves

minutiae of lash, flare
opening attracts
        glamour

            closing on

the curve of cheek, soft
worn particular
you glow within

        what eye?   what you?
        impossible

            portraiture's

                    attempt to
                    write you in

history balks at
new lines new
subject signs it
(generic

"love"

ℰ❧

this way photographic

            & aglow we climb, sun in broom, the long
slow daze of hillside langour where eyes graze the gold a
visual clamour full-scale desire's longing to tip

its hold on movement, moment into

                        act/ you

                            turn, laughter in your
gaze, the world

              rights itself, & sensibly we pace, pose as
only friends, these ruts worn deep by others' intent/   will the
dog still his rush after a thrown stick? (not the question, sweet
lure of broom's lash your accidental touch

           brimming, pausing

                       while eye wavers in the balance
                       wants

wills your face to turn its shine in wild astringent scent
& still the brass surround we rise to meet, wade through
histories of cheek, outrageous gold i'd heap you in

this stridency of high desire the brim of a hat, curve of your
lip mine tilts to meet, bee-quick —

the darting dog between, between …

would substance that elusive
"core" where your world
spins its axis all direction
measured by a *self:*

                    the way you tilt your brim
                    the way you pull me in

                         (historic non sequitur

would i's
exert such pull
without our wanting them
to?

               ℰ

now this photo/
graphing you a

                              water dance it glimmers brilliant
track incessant form diaphanous wing this light swarm being
draws, soft curve of cheek arm hair

                                 illumined white

you in a restaurant chair

under solid wood
the roof support encased
erased in wave
                   iota
                       (glint —

behind your face, not literal love shimmers its biosphere some instant
play i recognize in cheek, lash, light

                         holds us within it
                                 characteristic, i

see you deep in the unexpected, arms outstretched to wave
pure alabaster light or quartz there in your eye, hair rising off
your chair & into polar dazzle constellated in the where of you

small bear aplay on a floe just off   (the porch)   beyond
(Vesuvius)   & through the corner of your eyes

                              ferocious light

                              ℘ә

not myth, you
no more elemental than
the play of light an eye/my
particulars catch

      on yours, bare

            storying delight
                  no sleight of word

a tangled weft of pain
in Tunbridge Wells
Stoke Newington stones
you pass me
thick with your pulse

    psyche flags are flying
    their ragged past
    fragments of pattern

      almost indecipherable

          frog vocables of night
          chirp *us here, us here*

             (who?

.

caught by astilbe's flimsy presence in
the window pane

or you graph me in

                        your eyes' quick mercury smile the
shine the keeping words can't speak de-light de/cision   (click)
flickers
              between
                        a look & a word

                                           our histories
exclude, elude the exact shade of (blue?) (or green?) we balk at, eye-dentifying
whole oceans between

                        still the stream rhapsodic creaming
into light licks off-melodic the melody stays, sustained, plays lovelight's
variant in the wind a striped curtain makes of the room a pulse
illumined

              strays

                        across wood sweeping the day ship-
shape in the wake of you, meet

                        anything-goes writing a face in
the shade of a brim, eyes lifted out of pattern-wisdom, ship/ slip the knot we sorrow in,
desire cleft with attachment, left

                                           hanging

still on board, waking or breaking rhythm here we walk the course (our talk of course repeats to drum us in

                                   to want
                                   you (converse & particular, this-time-eyes

solo note)

                                           wild in the garden's late
light jingling dog licence bird euphoric opening salute head-on the long
flutter of our tongues' bipolar flick, and full

                           this tremor love is, all premise
promise, fold-
            over —

                           — no hold anywhere

ॐ

it's distinct, this
internal weather

you curled on my isolate
window seat, feet up out of
the rut regret's posted

    Rough Water ...

no one else could possibly cross

   ha, your voice with its innate
   equilibrium tilts my view

     finding the aperture
     opens me to you

        ℬ

caught you, graphic

       not in focus, slide off somewhere film
won't hold the pose a hat, a particular grace / fixate / love's
alchemical rush

      its very site a transit into

      (hue on hue the bay
       clear
        mist today

        . . .

      to keep us strange under one roof
      the look in an eye love fuses to
      arrives, it must

          from elsewhere, all

those memory banks we've pushed off from, unreeling other
harbours, ragged departures and their slow dissolve a tearing
white when continuity goes — *love* the feature we

              : hesitate

my a miss, mist
no more mine than

the distant bay dancing its heart out there in the blue
drift a shared transparency we reside where sheets slip
all along your thigh my fingers hot and homeless
drumming home — home is nothing, not the one
long shot we turn to wave/
                    waver into, un-

                                        done & shoreless in the

night's long-

                drawn

                                    (sigh)

TRACING THE CUT

Tracing The Cut

remains of two houses, chimney
foundered, the concrete body of
whose dreaming?

stone rent for smoke
paling into thin air

old MacDonald had a beach

> one pine in a
> place of ruins
> *mamu tsog sa*
> where *tsombus* dwell

& the water, & the water
long lengths of it lap at
granite's shoulder, lap-
lick at skinflakes, sand
dribbles

the splendour of light's appetite
eating up detail in this
dark fist of mountains

> we inhabit, momentary
> detail, a piece cut off from
> *détailler*, to cut (thoroughly

> _____PHAT_____

so light swims, language
opens its connect-
ing points, com-
panion in this
eating of light

. . .

opening anywhere underfoot
worn, water-washed & unremarkable
shingle, it's ankle-twist
lake stone time, ah

mica glints
hints of, crumbs of

      "opening door of the sky"

thunderheads ride the ridge
my body tipi pole
forget it holds up this cathedral well
we share, 6 beds or 6 damp heads
opening, 20 poles wide
empty-head companions in this

      changing our mind or
      it changes, all the time

. . .

down
　　　pour a
lightning constriction
thinking i
can't
　　　do what in what
　　　time? what i
in here?

hears the solid beat
lift, in a wavelike motion
wrist turn & lift the drum
fluid, of the heart's enlarging

　　　　　　　　　　. . .

　　　out there
　　　lake-wise
　　　succession of
　　　waves the wind
　　　plies

　　　　　　　(sudden loss is a cut
　　　　　　　insists on itself

　　　　　　　　　　a part
　　　　　　　　　　a parting

(she is no more here than

. . .

eyes' once clear focus
fades, refocus then on

evening impatiens a blur
vivid fuchsia catching last
light streaking down pebble path
                (distance viscid
up close brilliant
rubber squall jacket
a background

such colour
        (she'd want to paint
        he'd image it
        through the lens

a grace-note held
in attention, someone's
thought to set

        or no, just grace
        drops
        evenly all round

. . .

this supper hour's dank tarp
soft light, last burst of colour
shifts so quick to fade-
out eating up our
storied bodies gone
soft, gone lax cupping
warm evening's

     coffee or?
     tea for me please

a female eye for detail
flowers in the bush
amber eyes, throaty laugh

     you're the tea
     expert, how many
     bags?

indicating our still-intact
identities in body language we
linger, waiting for vesper

     (another whisper, faint
     sunday echo walking
     home in the quiet
        bless'd

     fold after fold in time's warp
     sand
        which'd —

. . .

empty, he says

the surface of a
still lake a sky
mirror

. . .

all night, all
day till afternoon, successive
waves crash wall
after wall of green
disintegrate, each
smash on stones'
thunk the resonant
well of the drum
we carry

        each particular
        step on shingle, glide
        of the solitary ones
        or the hummers, quick
        humorous ones, intent, the confirmed
        communicators against silence, or the light
        ones who like to
        stretch out on logs

gone listening
deep as the jagged chasms of moss
in ponderosa bark ravines

        ravenous, ponderous

so ghosts & gods throng the
familial body stuck in
time's warp

a ruin clung to, for memory's sake
the story the abandoned
mother-body fallen — fireweed, ghost wreath

circling back

      (coronary or suicide?

        breath on a mirror
        at this particular
        age, same age, same

tsombus, zombie fear
whips like wind rising
waves of after-shock

the story the body still
clinging

             __cut___

           . . .

"we make ourselves complicated"

Rinpoche in the *gompa*
yellow sail / swallowtail
large as a laugh
attaches itself to his sleeve

sitting simply "this
human body" vivid &
"at last attained"
                    (fuchsia perfect
fragile & changing
with each breath
                    (large as a laugh
                    & flutter-brief

wind-, lake-, pine-
mothers all round
tsombus, devas, pretas
all breath-beings & non-breath sky

offered thus

SOURCES

A Lost Book

"space activities": Charles Olson, "The Animate versus the Mechanical, and Thought" in A Bibliography on America, Proprioception, & Other Notes & Essays. (Bolinas: Four Seasons Foundation, 1974).

"one spoonful": Robin Blaser, "The Moth Poem," *The Holy Forest* (Toronto: Coach House Press, 1993).

"a series of takes": Marguerite Duras, "'An Act Against All Power'," *Duras by Duras* (San Francisco: City Lights, 1987).

Sea Shining Between

title page: Renée Vivien, *Poèmes de Renée Vivien*, vol. 1 (Paris: Librairie Alphonse Lemerre, 1923); Judy Grahn, *The Highest Apple* (Duluth, MN: Spinsters Ink, 1985).

"booking passage": Mary Barnard, *Sappho: A New Translation* (Berkeley: University of California Press, 1958).

"central to the periphery": H.D., "The Flowering of the Rod," "The Walls Do Not Fall," *Trilogy* (New York: New Directions, 1973).

"the approach re-approached ...": Luce Irigaray, trans. Catherine Porter, *This Sex Which Is Not One* (Ithaca: Cornell U.P., 1985).

"*the shape that grief takes*": Rachel Rose, *giving my body to science* (Montreal: McGill-Queen's U.P., 1999); Anne Pippin Burnett, *Three Archaic Poets: Archilochos, Alcaeus, Sappho* (London: Duckworth, 1983).

"crossing": Renée Vivien, *Poèmes de Renée Vivien*, vol. 1 (Paris: Librairie Alphonse Lemerre, 1923); Renée Vivien, trans. Margaret Porter & Catharine Kroger, *The Muse of the Violets* (Tallahassee, FL: Naiad Press, 1977).

"passage between": Nicole Brossard, *La Nuit verte du Parc Labyrinth* (Laval: Les Editions trois, 1992).

"in the current": Hélène Cixous & Mireille Calle-Gruber, trans. Eric Prenowitz, *rootprints* (New York, London: Routledge, 1997).

"(is love enough?)": Olga Broumas, *Perpetua* (Port Townsend: Copper Canyon Press, 1989); Mary Barnard, *Sappho: A New Translation* (Berkeley: University of California Press, 1958)